PFALZGALERIE KAISERSLAUTERN

Passages – Übergänge

Elena Gaputyte
Rosie Leventon
Diane Maclean
Christine Merton

4. März bis 16. April 1990

Folgende Institute und Firmen haben diese Ausstellung finanziell oder durch Sachspenden unterstützt:

The British Council, London

Buhler & Sohn, Kaiserslautern

German Tourist Facilities, London

Hatcham Rubber Ltd., London

Philips Licht GmbH, Hamburg

Metallgesellschaft AG Frankfurt

Vorwort

Die vier britischen Künstlerinnen, als Malerinnen oder Bildhauerinnen ausgebildet, unterschiedlicher Herkunft, verschiedenen Alters und in ihren Denkansätzen und künstlerischen Aussagen nur bedingt vergleichbar, sind zunächst durch ihre gemeinsame Zugehörigkeit zu einer größeren Gruppe, der Londoner Künstlervereinigung „Diameter" verbunden. Daß gerade sie sich zu einer gemeinsamen Ausstellung zusammenfanden, versteht sich aus ihrem Anliegen, nicht mit Hilfe von Pinsel und Leinwand oder Meißel und Marmor einem privaten Gefühl oder einem subjektiven Schönheitsideal Ausdruck zu verleihen, sondern dem Betrachter etwas mitzuteilen, was auch ihn betrifft, oder betreffen könnte, ihn teilnehmen zu lassen an Vorstellungen, Überlegungen, Gedanken, die Bezug nehmen auf unser Leben, unser Lebensgefühl, unser Dasein und seine Bedingungen. Gemeinsam ist den vier Künstlerinnen ihr Bemühen, den Betrachter in ihren Kunstraum einzubeziehen, ihm damit einen neuen Denkraum zu erschließen.

Elena Gaputyte, Rosie Leventon, Diane Maclean und Christine Merton haben jeweils einen Raum der Pfalzgalerie nach ihren Vorstellungen gestaltet und thematisiert. Es sind vier Rauminstallationen sehr unterschiedlicher Art entstanden, aus Materialien wie Holz, Papier, Stoff und Elementen wie Wasser, Licht und Wind, begehbare, erlebbare Environments mit Wegen, Wasserläufen, Behausungen und Altären; Passagen oder „Übergänge" von einem engagierten Denkansatz in plastische Form verwandelt. Ihre Arbeiten sind beides, konzentrierte Form und transformiertes Gedankengebäude, und, bei aller Lesbarkeit ihrer Zeichen und Symbole, ihrer dreidimensionalen Präsenz, nicht allein von ihrer Äußerlichkeit her zu entschlüsseln.

Frühere Arbeiten von Elena Gaputyte, die aus Litauen stammt, und von Christine Merton, die in Deutschland geboren wurde, waren bereits in Berlin, in Kaiserslautern (1983) und Frankfurt zu sehen. Sie, die ihre künstlerische Ausbildung noch in Deutschland begonnen hatten, sind in England heimisch geworden und haben sich in die Londoner Kunstszene integriert. Mit anderen Künstlerinnen zusammen gründeten sie 1985 die Gruppe „Diameter", in der die unterschiedlichsten künstlerischen Ansätze repräsentiert sind. Da nicht die Darstellung einer bunt gemischten freien Künstlervereinigung hier angestrebt war, sondern eine in sich schlüssige, vom Ansatz her vergleichbare Präsentation, wurden diese vier, vorwiegend im plastischen Bereich arbeitenden Künstlerinnen ausgewählt, wobei es für Rosie Leventon und Diane Maclean, die in ihrer Heimat schon längst zu den anerkannten Künstlern gehören, die erste Ausstellung auf dem „Kontinent" ist.

Gisela Fiedler-Bender

Übergänge

Eine Ausstellung von vier Künstlerinnen

„Wird es eine Zeit der Frauen geben, oder werden wir sterben?" – Ian McEwan

I. Das Thema

„Denn Bleiben ist nirgends." – Rainer Maria Rilke

Wenn wir in der Sprache des Volkes sprechen, bringen wir das Persönliche ins Mythische ein, verschlüsseln wir die Ereignisse des eigenen Lebens in allgemeine Überlieferung und verwandeln das Zufällige und Rätselhafte in Modelle und Bedeutungen. Aus der weitgespannten Dialektik von Sprache und Mythos entsteht die Gestalt unseres Lebens –, mit den Worten Ernst Cassirers *„die großen Strukturen der mythischen und sprachlichen Sphären, wie sie während langer Entwicklungsphasen durch die gleichen geistigen Motive bestimmt und weitergeführt werden."* Im Zentrum dieser dynamischen Wechselwirkung steht die Fähigkeit des Denkens in Metaphern, durch welche ein Ding oder eine Erfahrung durch etwas ganz anderes, Unterschiedliches bezeichnet wird. Aus der Metapher ist beides entstanden, Sprache und Mythos; was die Sprache betrifft, so ist sie die Umsetzung von Erfahrung in symbolischen Klang, und so kann die „einfachste mythische Form ... nur durch die Kraft der Verwandlung entstehen, die einen bestimmten Eindruck aus dem Bereich des Gewöhnlichen, Alltäglichen, Profanen entnimmt und diesen auf die Ebene des „Heiligen" hebt, in die Sphäre mythisch-religiöser Bedeutung.

Diese große Vision des Ursprungs von Sprache, Mythos und Religion kann mit der Anschauung des dialektischen Materialismus vom Entstehen der Kunst in Einklang gebracht werden, wie es Ernst Fischer so treffend ausgedrückt hat: Kunst *„ist eine Form von Arbeit",* durch die der Mensch von der Natur Besitz ergreift, indem er sie umformt. Der Mensch träumt auch von magischer Herrschaft über die Natur, von der Fähigkeit, die Dinge zu verändern und ihnen durch magische Bedeutung neue Form zu geben. Der Mensch ist von Anfang an ein Magier. Hinsichtlich des Schaffens von Kunst sprechen wir immer von „Arbeit" und von „Arbeiten". Sich etwas vorstellen meint umformen: das ist der erste schöpferische Akt. Die Menschheit hat sich Zeit überall in Begriffen des Räumlichen gedacht, in dem wir existieren. *„Was bedeuten Tage? Tage sind, wo wir leben";* wo wir leben, bedingt das Sosein unseres Lebens. Und gerade so, wie wir das Land vermessen, Flüsse und Küsten kartographisch festlegen, Meere und Himmel erfassen, um dem Unendlichen des Raumes Gestalt und Form zu geben, um uns darin selbst zu bestimmen und unseren Behausungen eine Identität zu geben, so markieren wir auch unser Leben mit sinnvollen Augenblicken, veranstalten Feiern und Zeremonien, um unseren verschiedenen und privaten Schicksalen Form und Gemeinsamkeit zu geben.

Das Leben als Reise ist eines der ältesten Bilder in der Geschichte menschlicher Vorstellung. In vielen Mythen ist es eine Reise ohne Ende, denn der Tod ist nur das Tor zu weiteren Wagnissen, ein Übergang von einem Dasein ins andere, und unsere Geburt ist *„nur ein Schlaf und ein Vergessen",* ein Schritt über die Schwelle aus einem früheren Zustand. So ist denn unser Dasein stets ein Übergang; und so sehen wir uns als Nomaden der Zeit, indem wir unsere Gebiete, die *„Wüsten unermeßlicher Ewigkeit",* wie Marvell sagt, durchqueren oder über weite Meere fahren. Es hat immer schon auch andere, mehr ortsgebundene Vorstellungen und Allegorien gegeben: Mythenschreiber und Philosophen, Künstler und Dichter, die ihre Visionen als Lebensweg, symbolisiert durch Täler, Flüsse und Straßen, verdeutlicht haben.

Es gibt keine Kultur ohne Riten der Übergänge und schon immer in der Geschichte und tatsächlich vor der Geschichte, gehörte es zu den ersten Aufgaben der Kunst, Idole und Zauberformeln zu schaffen, die jene Zeremonien begleiten, und die Geschichten, die ihren Sinn erklären, immer wieder zu erzählen und, wenn nötig, neu zu erfinden. (Wie der Etnograph E. B. Taylor im 19. Jahrhundert bemerkt: *„Der Mythos kann gleichförmiger sein als die Geschichte.")* In profanen und materialistischen Zeiten mögen solche Hinweise unerkannt bleiben. Aber sogar die verschiedenen Realismen, die unsere abendländische Kultur schon so lange prägen (z.B. die bürgerliche und erzählende Malerei, der Roman, oder der Film) und die den analytischen Zielen sukzessiver positivistischer Aufklärung gedient haben, sind vom Mythos strukturiert und durch die allgemeine Erfahrung der Rasse und der Rituale geformt, die sie begleiten. Denn auch das analytische Auge ist menschlich; falls das, was es wahrnimmt, ein Bild in einem ständigen Chaos von Bildern ist, etwas schöpferisch Imaginiertes, bewirkt durch die Kraft des Geistes über die vorgegebene Welt: *„Das Auge ist Teil der Vernunft."* Und es wirkt innerhalb dieser Kultur, indem es sich ihrer räumlichen, zeitlichen und geistigen Landkarten bedient, bewegt von ihrer Geschichte, berührt von ihrem Glauben, sogar wenn es versuchen sollte, deren Gültigkeit zu bestätigen oder zu bestreiten.

In diesem Jahrhundert sind andere Kunstformen entstanden, elementarer, mehr aufs Ursprüngliche zielend, wobei alte Rituale mit neuem Leben erfüllt werden; abstrakter, indem versucht wird, in Farbe und Form sichtbare Zeichen unsichtbarer Realitäten zu finden, mehr auf geistige Weise, auf der Suche nach adäquat Symbolischem in unserem Lebensgefühl und Todesbewußtsein. Viele Künstler haben auf die schrecklichen Erschütterungen der heutigen Zeit mit der Weigerung geantwortet, gefällige, das bloß Sichtbare und Greifbare darstellende Werke zu schaffen. In der Verweigerung von Dada haben sie die neuen Anfänge einer Kunst der Gebärde, der Vermittlung von Idee und Erinnerung gefunden. Der Dada-Bewegung galt die Negation aller Negationen durch den Weltkrieg verkörpert, mit den Worten von Max Ernst war es *„ein rebellisches Aufbegehren von vitaler Energie und Raserei, daher die Absurdität, die ganze ungeheure Schweinerei jenes idiotischen Krieges."* Heute wissen wir von anderen Übeln, genauso groß oder noch größer als die des Krieges, und darum fordern wir eine Kunst, die Wut und Abscheu nicht kennt, dafür Mitleid und Kummer mit umfaßt und sich gegen alle Verzweiflung wendet. In einer Epoche geistiger Zersplitterung, von Glaubensverlust und unbegreiflicher Gewalt, schrecklicher Verwirrungen und Verdrängungen ist es Aufgabe der Kunst, neue Rituale zu schaffen, die unseren Lebensweg sinnvoll wiedergeben. Wir leben in solch einer Zeit: das menschliche Miteinander ist zerstört, seine geschichtlich gewachsene Kultur zerstreut, die Sprachen verboten, an den Rand gedrängt oder vergessen, die schönen mythischen Strukturen, die die Religionen bedingen, dienen zur Rechtfertigung von Fanatismus, Ächtung und Ausgrenzung; das zarte Gewebe des Glaubens ist zu einem böswilligen Dogma degeneriert. Aggressive Anmaßung, rücksichtslose Verschwendung und Zerstörung von globalem Ausmaß, der Triumph von Habgier und Egoismus im wechselseitigen Miteinander, böse, unbestimmte Ängste und Verwirrungen sind Kennzeichen dieser Zeit. In einer solchen Zeit kann die Kunst eine Weise des Erinnerns sein, die uns an das gemahnt, was sonst vergessen werden könnte: indem sie bezeugt und feiert, beschreibt sie Übergänge und markiert so die Stationen unseres gemeinsamen Schicksals.

II. Die Künstlerinnen und das Werk

"Trouve une langue; – Du reste, tout parole étant idée, le temps d'un langage universel viendra! ... Cette langue sera de l'âme pour l'âme, résumant tout, parfums, sons, couleurs ... Ces pöetes seront! Quand sere brisé l'infini servage de la femme ... La femme trouvera de l'inconnu!" –
Arthur Rimbaud

Etwas bewegt sich in der heutigen Kunst. Es hat zu tun mit dem Verzicht auf individuelle Ausdrucksweise, es ist eher eine neue Einstellung zu den Materialien der Kunst denn ihre bloße Beherrschung. Es ist ein komplexes Phänomen das ich hier andeute, schwer zu definieren. Eine Bewegung in dem Sinne wie etwa eine Unterwasserströmung eine Bewegung ist: Manifestation von Energie. Einer der ersten, die einen solchen Energieimpuls freisetzten, war Marcel Duchamp mit seinem Verzicht auf die konventionelle, bloß auf die „Retina" bezogene Kunst, war seine andere Vorgehensweise um zu entdecken, und seine Objektbestimmung war der Schlüssel dazu. In seiner Grundeinstellung gegenüber dem elementar Stofflichen der umgebenden Wirklichkeit wie in seinen Aktionen, die Situationen schufen und Teilnahme bewirkten, war Beuys in unseren Tagen ein dynamischer Vermittler solcher metaphysischen Energien.

Auf unterschiedliche Weise und an verschiedenen Orten sind gewisse Künstler dabei, diese Rolle zu übernehmen, teils als Mittler, teils als Magier: Um gleichsam ein Hörender zu werden angesichts des Schweigens der Geschichte, Deuter von Sinnzeichen, Stifter von Sakramenten. Solchen Künstlern wird ihr Tun zur Performance, eine beziehungsreiche Präsentation von Objekten, eine Aktion, welche die Orte, an denen sie stattfindet, vorübergehend heraushebt. Ein Künstler, der sich auf solche Weise engagiert, ist nicht länger mehr nur ein Schöpfer besonderer Dinge, sondern bewirkt Ereignisse und Feiern.

Nach der Aktion zieht der Künstler weiter. Die von ihm verwendeten Materialien sind oft elementar und ursprünglich, zerbrechlich und vergänglich: Lehm, Wasser, Luft und Feuer, Kieselsteine, gefundene Dinge, Holz, Tuch, Papier; die Markierungen und Zeichen sind elementar und nicht von Dauer: Kratzer und Farbflecken, Sgraffiti, Lichter, einfache Wörter. Die Fotografie, bei der das Licht die Erinnerungen auf der Platte festhält, tatsächliche Spuren vorübergehender Augenblicke und Dinge, ist oftmals ein unbestechlicher Zeuge und erinnert eindringlich an die Aktion und ihre flüchtigen Objekte.

Jede der Künstlerinnen, die sich in dieser Ausstellung zusammengetan haben, verfährt auf diese Weise: Gemeinsam schaffen sie im Geist der Zeit. Jede von ihnen ist bestrebt, Bildhaftes zu gestalten, das uns über das Werk selbst hinausführt, Werke gleichsam als Einstieg in Erfahrungsbereiche des Unsichtbaren. Diese Arbeiten sind natürlich nicht malerisch bildhaft, sie ahmen nicht irgend etwas nach: In ihnen sind Gegenstand und Abbildung eins. Indem sie die beschriebenen elementaren Materialien der neuen Kunst verwenden (einer Kunst, die Ausdrucksweisen und Absichten des Frühgeschichtlichen und Ursprünglichen wieder aufgreift, also aus alten Quellen schöpft), wirken diese Stücke gleichermaßen als andeutende Zeichen und Beschwörung. Sie sind natürlich Teilhabende an einer Zeremonie, Mitwirkende an einem Akt vitaler Erinnerung.

Christine Mertons Zelte lassen an den nomadischen Charakter unseres Lebenswegs denken, an die Erde gebunden, dann weiterziehend: Abbilder der fragilen Behausung der ruhelos wandernden Seele. Diane Macleans hinweisende Erinnerungen an Seereisen, Klippen, Pfade und Bergpässe, sind Beschwörungen wirklicher Reisen als Symbole allgemein menschlicher Übergänge. Aus einer Art spirituellen Archäologie erschafft Rosie Leventon ein Theater geistiger Neuorientierung, in dem alte Riten zu neuen Formen und Abläufen finden, doch immer mittels alter Mysterien. Im Spiel von Oberfläche und Tiefe macht sie Grenzzeichen begreifbar, einen Durchgang von einem Zustand in den anderen, von Oben und Unten, von Hell und Dunkel. Elena Gaputytes schöne Arrangements aus Licht und Objekt, ihre sorgsame Präsentation, sind Akte der Bestätigung und Sühne zugleich. Ihre Arbeiten gemahnen an die schrecklichen Ereignisse des letzten Krieges und dessen Nachwirkungen; bei aller scheinbaren Ausweglosigkeit rufen sie im „flackernden Licht" nach Gerechtigkeit, Mitleid und Hoffnung. In ihrem Miteinander bezeugen die Arbeiten dieser vier Künstlerinnen ein vielfältiges und bemerkenswertes Faktum: Wir sind aufgefordert, uns eigene Vorstellungen hinsichtlich ihrer imaginierten Räume zu machen, innezuhalten auf unserem Weg um nachzudenken, zu erinnern und zu feiern.

Mel Gooding

Passages

An exhibition created by four woman artists

Shall there be womanly times, or shall we die? – Ian McEwan

I The Theme

For staying is nowhere. – Rainer Maria Rilke

Making *speech* in "the language of the tribe", we inscribe the personal within the mythic, codify the events of the individual life into a common lore, and transfigure the random and the unintelligible into pattern and meaning. Out of the great dialectic of language and myth is generated the shape of our lives: this is how, in Ernst Cassirer's words, "... the great structures of the mythic and the linguistic realms, respectively, are determined and guided through long periods of their development by the same spiritual motives." At the centre of this dynamic interaction is the faculty of *metaphorical thinking,* by which one thing or experience is apprehended in terms of something other and categorically different. Out of metaphor is born both language and myth: for just as language is the transposition of experience into symbolising sound, so can "the simplest mythical form ... arise only by virtue of a transformation which removes a certain impression from the realm of the ordinary, the everyday and profane, and lifts it to the level of the 'holy', the sphere of mythico-religious 'significance' ".

This grand vision of the origins of language, myth and religion can be reconciled with that dialectical materialist view of the origins of art so eloquently expressed by Ernst Fischer: art "is a form of work", by which "man takes possession of the natural by transforming it ... Man also dreams of working magic upon nature, of being able to change objects and give them new form by magic means. This is the equivalent in the imagination of what work means in reality. Man is, from the outset, a magician." We speak continuously of the art activity as "work", and of its products as "works". To imagine is to transform: it is the primary creative act.

Humankind has everywhere thought of time in terms of the spaces in which we have our being: *"What are days for? Days are where we live";* where we live provides the image of our life itself. And just as we mark out the land, map the rivers and the coasts, and chart the seas and skies, to bring the infinities of space into shape and form, to site ourselves and give identity to our habitations, so too we mark our journey with moments of significance, make celebrations and ceremonies to give shape and common habitude to our various and private destinies.

Life as a journey is one of the oldest images in the history of human imaginings. In many myths it is a journey that has no ending, for death is but an entrance to further adventures, a passage across from this condition to another, and our birth is "but a sleep and a forgetting", an entry across the threshold from some previous state. Our existence, then, is at every moment a transition; we picture ourselves as Time's nomads, traversing our quarter of what Marvell called "desarts of vast Eternity", or voyaging across unmeasured seas. There have been more local and homely images and allegories; mythmakers and philosophers, and the artists and poets who make tangible their visions, have imaged the universal way through valleys, along rivers and roads.

There is no culture without rites of passage, and throughout history (and indeed before "history") the primary functions of art have been to make the sacred signs and incantations that accompany those ceremonies, and to tell and re-tell, and to re-invent when necessary, the tales that encode their meanings. (As the nineteenth century ethnographer E.B. Tyler remarked: "Myth may be more uniform than history.") In secular and materialist times these purposes may be disguised. But even the various *Realisms,* which have dominated our Western culture for so long, (domestic and narrative painting, the novel, or the fictional movie, for examples), and which have served the analytic purposes of successive positivist enlightenments, are structured by myth and shaped by the common experience of the race and the rituals that attend it. For the analytic eye is also human; if what it perceives is an image among a continuous welter of images, what it *comprehends* is something creatively imagined, generated by the working of the mind upon the world as given: "The eye is part of the mind." And it operates within its culture, utilising its spatial, temporal and spiritual cartographies, affected by its histories, touched by its beliefs, even as it may seek to confirm or deny their validities.

There have arisen in this century other forms of art: more elemental, drawing upon the primitive, enacting in new ways ancient rituals; more abstract, attempting to find visible metaphors, in colour and form, for invisible realities; more spiritual, searching for some symbolism adequate to our sense of life and consciousness of death. Many artists have responded to the terrible convulsions of the modern era with a rejection of those art-objects that complacently celebrate the visible and the tangible. In the negations of Dada they have found the new beginnings of an art of gesture, of placement, of idea and evocation. For Dada was a negation of the negation represented by the Great War: in Max Ernst's words, it was "... a rebellious upsurge of vital energy and rage; it resulted from the absurdity, the whole immense *Schweinerei* of that imbecilic war." We know now of other evils, as great or greater than those of that war, and we have required an art that goes beyond anger and disgust to encompass pity and sorrow, and that treats against despair.

In an epoch of spiritual fragmentation and of lost beliefs, of incomprehensible violences, of terrible dislocations and displacements, it becomes necessary for art to enact the rituals by which we make sense of our passage through the world. We live in such a time: when communities are destroyed, their historical cultures scattered and their languages forbidden, marginalised or forgotten; when the beautiful mythic structures that sustain religions have become the justification of bigotries and cruel proscriptions and exclusions; when subtle patterns of faith have degenerated into malevolent dogma. It is a period marked by aggressive assertiveness, mindless wastefulness and destruction on a global scale, by the triumph of greed and selfishness over interdependence and mutual aid in social life, and by dark subjective fears and confusions. In such a time art may be a form of remembering, reminding us of what might otherwise be forgot: in its witness and celebration it describes the passages and marks the stations of our common fate.

II The Artists and the Work

"Trouver une langue; – Du reste, toute parole étant idée, le temps d'un langage universel viendra! ... Cette langue sera de l'âme pour l'âme, résumant tout, parfums, sons, couleurs ... Ces poëtes seront! Quand sere brisé l'infini servage de la femme ... La femme trouvera de l'inconnu!" – Arthur Rimbaud

Something is going on in modern art. It is something to do with the abnegation of personal expressiveness, something to do with another attitude towards the materials of art than that of mastery over them. It is a complex phenomenon that I am hinting at, elusive of description. It is not a movement, except in the sense that an underwater current is a movement, a manifestation of energy. One of the primal generators of this impulse of energy was the creative project of Duchamp, which included his renunciation of conventional and "retinal" art, his turning to other activities as means to discovery, his designation of objects as keys to revelation. Beuys, in his approach to elemental materials and the givens of the circumstantial world, and in his actions as a maker of situations and interventions, has been a dynamic transmitter of this metaphysical energy in recent times.

In diverse ways in different places, certain artists have elected to take on this role, part medium, part magician; to become *listeners* to the silences in history, interpreters of signs, enactors of sacrament. For such artists the work becomes a performance, a significant presentation of objects, an *action* temporarily marking and transforming the places in which it takes place. The artist thus engaged is no longer a maker of privileged objects, but a maker of events and ceremonies. The action made, the artist moves on. The materials this artist uses are often elemental and rudimentary, or fragile and transient: clay, water, air and fire, pebbles, found objects, wood, cloth, paper; the marks and signs are elementary and impermanent: scratchings and stainings, wall drawings, lights, simple words. Photography, created of the memory that light leaves on the plate, the actual trace of past moments, things passed away, is often a crucial record and poignant reminder of the action and its fugitive objects.

Each of the artists who have together made this manifestation is of this kind: collaborators with each other and with the spirit of the time. Each of them is concerned to make images that take us beyond the work itself, images that will act as thresholds to domains of experience beyond the visible. These works are not, of course, pictorial, they are not *imitations* of something else: in them, object and image are one. Using the elemental materials of that new art I have just described, (an art that recapitulates the modes and purposes of the prehistoric and the primitive, that draws on ancient sources), these pieces work by intimation and evocation.

They are, of course, components of a ceremony, adjuncts to an act of vital remembrance. Merton's tents remind us of our nomadic journey, touching the earth here, moving on; they are images of the fragile housing of the migratory soul. Maclean's evocations of sea voyages, of cliffs, pathways and passes, transfigure memories of actual journeys into symbols of the universal human passage. Out of a kind of spiritual archaeology Leventon creates a theatre of spiritual reclamation, in which ancient rites are found new forms and circumstances, but which use the matter of the ancient mysteries. In the play between surface and depth she apprehends a liminal metaphor, a transparent doorway from one condition to another, from above to below, from daylight to darkness. Gaputyte's beautiful arrangements of lights and objects, her careful presentations, are acts of witness and expiation. Her works recollect the dreadful events of the last War and its aftermath: they cry, in a flickering light, for justice, or at least pity and hope against the odds. Placed together the works of these four women artists constitute a complex and remarkable event: we are invited to make our own contemplative progress through the spaces they have imagined, pausing on our way for reflection, memory and celebration.

Mel Gooding, Barnes, January 1990

Notes and references

McEwan's question is asked in "Or Shall We Die?" an oratorio by Ian McEwan and Michael Berkeley (1983).
Rilke is quoted from The First Elegy: *"Denn Bleiben ist nirgends."*
"... the language of the tribe" is a phrase from Mallarmé.
Ernst Cassirers' great essay, "Language and Myth" was first published in German in 1923.
Ernst Fischer is quoted from "The Necessity of Art. A Marxist Approach" first published in Dresden in 1959 as "Von der Notwendigkeit der Kunst".
"What are days for?..." is from the poem by Philip Larkin.
E.B. Tyler's "Primitive Culture" was published in 1871.
Max Ernst is quoted by Uwe M. Schneede (ed.) "The Essential Max Ernst" (1972).
Rimbaud's prophetic words are from the letter to Paul Demeny, May 15, 1871.

☐ = in der Ausstellung

Elena Gaputyte

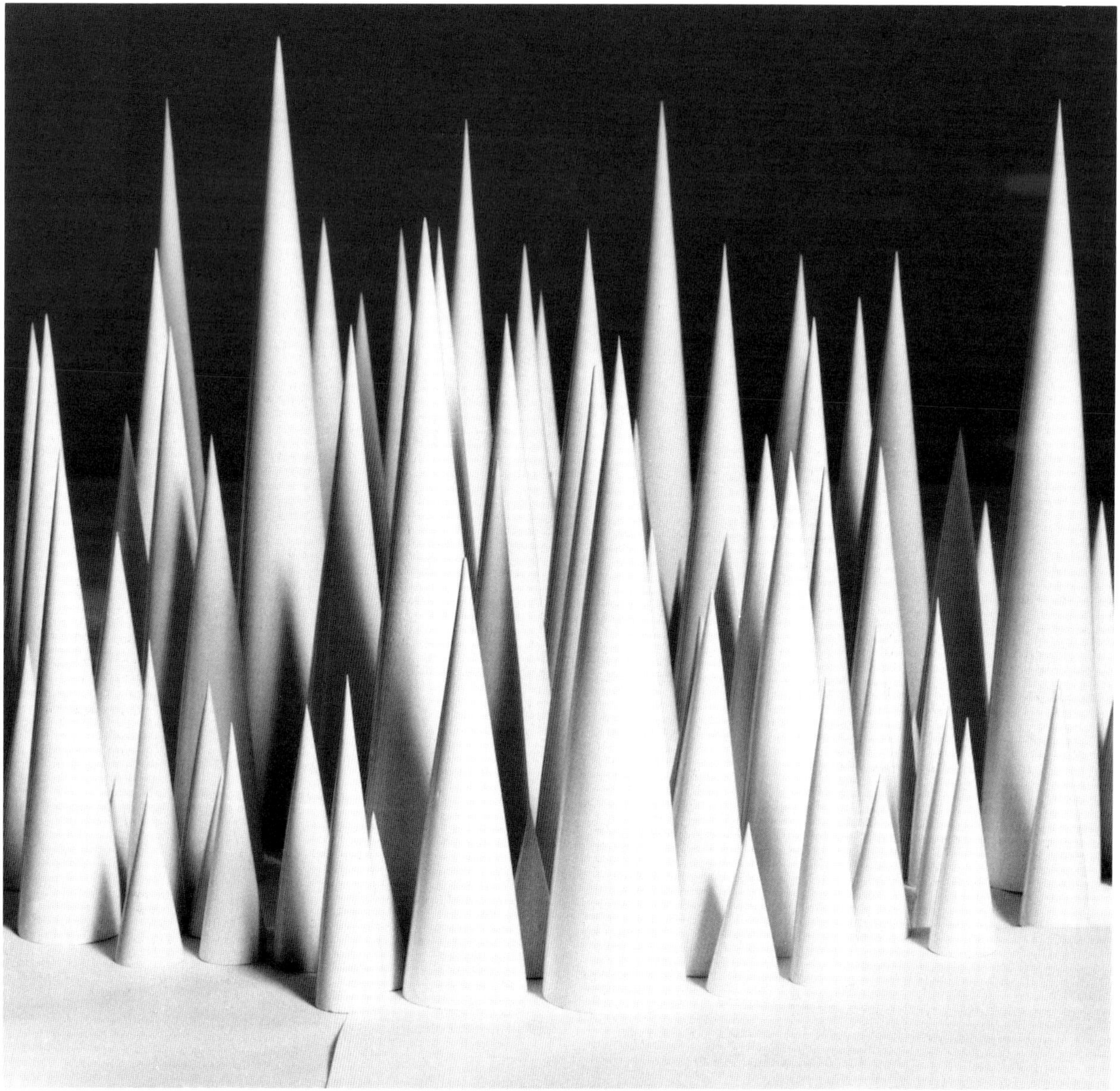

☐ Beyond the arctic circle – in memory of the Trofimovsk Victims 1989/90
100 Kegel, Holz, weiß lasiert
Höhe: 10 - 58 cm

☐ Beyond the arctic circle (Detail) – in memory of the Trofimovsk Victims, 1989/90

Lord's prayer I, 1978
Paros
Paros – Marmor, Sand
Ø 150 cm

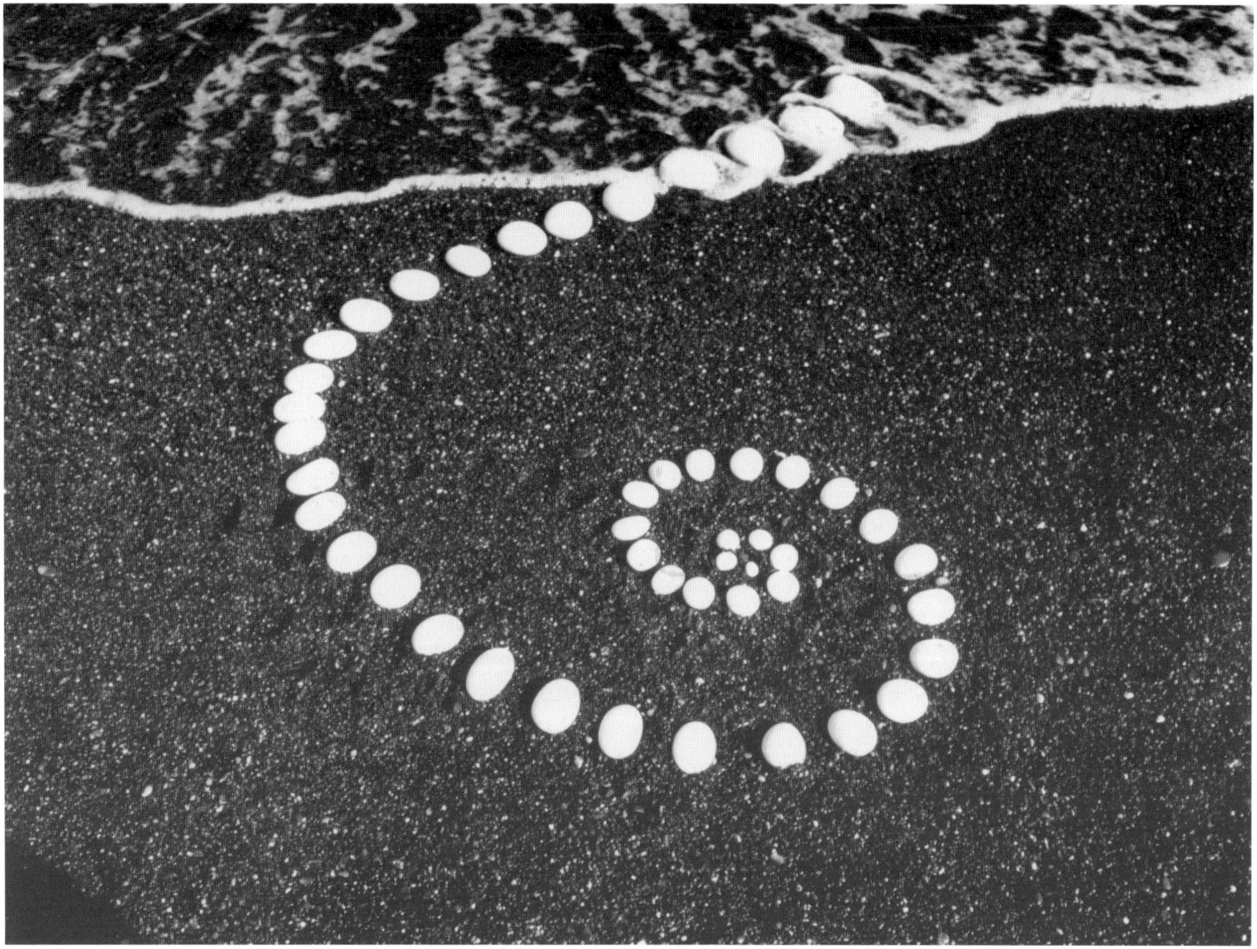

Lord's prayer II, 1978
Santorin
Paros – Marmor, Lavasand
∅ 250 cm

Calendar of my childhood – November, 1981
Eichenholz, Aluminium, Zweige
108 x 122 x 122 cm

Calendar of my childhood – March, 1981
Eichenholz, Aluminium, Erde
108 x 122 x 122 cm

Lord's prayer III, 1984
Berlin Kreuzberg
Paros Marmor, Berliner Mauer

Silent Witness, 1984
Anhalter Bahnhof, Berlin
100 Lichter
∅ 400 cm

In memory of the world war II dead, 1985
Albion Studios, London
560 Lichter
300 x 700 cm

Prophecy – 50 years on, 1989
Richard Demarco Gallery, Edinburgh
500 Lichter
Ø 450 cm

ELENA GAPUTYTE

1927	geboren in Litauen
	lebt in London
1946 - 48	Studium der Kunstgeschichte an der Universität Freiburg
1946 - 48	Kunstgewerbeschule Freiburg
1949 - 50	Ecole des Beaux Arts, Montreal
1951 - 52	Ontario College of Art, Toronto
1953 - 56	Academie des Beaux Arts, Paris
1960	Einrichtung der Sail Loft Gallery in St. Ives, bis 1964 deren Leiterin
1960	Französischer Staatspreis, Paris
1964 - 77	Leiterin der Skulpturen-Abteilung am Digby Stuart College, London University
1967 - 69	Hammersmith College of Art, London
1968 - 76	Ausstellungsleiterin am Digby Stuart College, London University
1969	Prüfungsbeauftragte für Kunsthandwerk am Institute of Education, London University
1969	Sachverständige für Skulpturen am Digby Stuart College, London University
1971 - 78	Jurymitglied der Pollyfille School Art Competition, London
1973	Preis des Arts Council of Great Britain
1974 - 75	Gast-Künstlerin an der Chelsea School of Art, London, Abschluß als Magister
1975	Erster Preis des Arts Council of Great Britain und der Easter Arts Association. Open air Competition, Key Theatre, Petersborough
1976	Dozentin an der London University
1978 - 81	Beauftragte für den Fachausschuß Kunst an der London University
1981	Beendigung der Lehrtätigkeit
1984	Gastkünstlerin im Künstlerhaus Berlin
1985	Gründungsmitglied der Künstlergruppe Diameter

EINZELAUSSTELLUNGEN

1961	The Gallery, Penzance, Cornwall
1962	Sail Loft Gallery, St. Ives, Cornwall
1963	Kidderminster Museum and Art Gallery, Kidderminster
1965	The Upper Grosvenor Galleries, London
1971	Balsekas Museum, Chicago, USA
1973	Marjorie Parr Gallery, London
1973	Romuva, Hüttenfeld, BRD
1973	The David Paul Gallery, Chichester
1981	LYC Museum and Art Gallery, Cumbria

1982	Vohrumhaus, Peine, BRD
1983	The Place Theatre, London (Foyer)
1983	Ciurlionis Gallery, Chicago, USA
1984 - 85	Berliner Mauer und Anhalter Bahnhof, West Berlin
1984	Manta Rota, Portugal
1985	Albion Studios, London – "Memories of war"
1985	Centro Pastorale "Mons. G. Carraro", Verona, Italien
1985	Riverside Studios, London
1986	Thiepval, Somme, Frankreich, 1. Juli 1986, Performance und Video „To all who suffered and died on the Somme"
1986	St. Davis, Wales, Bishop's Palace, Fishguard Music Festival
1986	Battersea Arts Gallery, London
1987	Unit 7 Gallery, London, (mit Rosie Leventon)
1989	The Richard Demarco Gallery, Edinburgh
1989	Reclaim the City Art Project, Glasgow

GRUPPENAUSSTELLUNGEN

1953	Exposition des Etudiants Internationale, Sorbonne, Paris
1954 - 56	Salon des Independants, Paris
1954	Exposition Galerie des Beaux Arts, Paris
1960	Steps Gallery, St. Ives, Cornwall
1960 - 63	Verschiedene Ausstellungen in der Sail Loft Gallery, St. Ives, Cornwall; Edward Passmore Gallery, Newlyn, Cornwall und Penwith Gallery, St. Ives, Cornwall
1962 - 64	Musée d'art Modern, Le Club International Feminin, Paris
1962	Rawinsky Gallery, London
1963	Centre Charles Peguy, London
1964	Muriel Beach-Thomas Gallery, Burford, Oxfordshire
1964 - 70	Thames Gallery, Eton; Bear Lane Gallery, Oxford; Leicester Galleries, London; Quantas Gallery, London; Ely House University Press, London; Drian Galleries, London; Piccadilly Galleries, London; South London Art Gallery, London
1971	Canada House Gallery, London; Commonwealth Institute Galleries, London; Ellingham Mills, Suffolk
1974	Circle Gallery, Croydon
1975	Wiggins Teape, London (Inner Eye Group)
1975	Commonwealth Book Fair, New Zealand House, London
1976	Abbot Hall Gallery, Kendal, Cumbria; Minories, Colchester
1977	Action Space, London
1979	Louvain-la-Neuve University, Belgien; Amnesty Int. Skulpturen-Ausstellung, Bristol Cathedral; Amnesty Int. Skulpturen-Ausstellung, St. Paul's, London
1982 - 83	"Prophecy and Vision", Wanderausstellung Arnolfini Gallery, Bristol, Glasgow, London and Londonderry

1984	Westminster Cathedral, London
1986	Battersea Arts Gallery, London, "British Women Artists Diary 1987"
1987	Riverside Studios, London
1987	Fulham Palace, Riverside Artists
1988	Pitt Rivers Museum, Oxford, 'Gathering Rites', Installation
1988	Litauen Art '88, Wanderausstellung Toronto, Los Angeles, Cleveland, Washington, Rochester
1988	Litauische Künstler im Exil, Wanderausstellung Vilnius, Klaipeda, Kaunas
1989	Litauische Kunst '89, Chicago
1989	The Royal National Rose Gardens, St. Albans, Herts, Installation
1990	"My Faith", Ciurlionis Gallery, Chicago, USA
1990	"Passages – Übergänge" Installationen und Skulpturen (mit Christine Merton, Diane Maclean und Rosie Leventon), Pfalzgalerie Kaiserslautern

PUBLIKATIONEN

The Painter und Sculptor, 1961 Nr. 2;
Apollo, Januar 1962;
Lithuanian Days USA, März 1963, Arts Reviev, 23. September 1964;
Arts Review, 30. Oktober 1965;
Arts Review Vol. XVI;
Cornish Review, Sommer 1966;
Nemunas 1968 Nr. 5 Lithuana; Art and Antiques Weekly, 16. Mai 1970;
Prophecy and Vision, Ausstellungskatalog 1982;
Metmenys, 1984, 24 Seiten illustrierter Artikel, USA; FAN, Vol. 2 Nr. 1, 1985;
The Tate Gallery, St. Ives 1939-64, Katalog 1985;
Aidai, Los Angeles, 1989

Rosie Leventon

ROSIE LEVENTON

1946	geboren in Bath
	lebt in London
1974 - 75	Studium der chinesischen Archäologie und Sprache an der London University
1976 - 79	Croydon College of Art
1979 - 80	Post graduate an der St. Martins School of Art, London
1979 - 82	Lehrtätigkeit in Surrey
1982	Gastdozentin am Croydon College of Art
1985	Gastdozentin am Cardiff College of Art
1986	Gastdozentin am Stourbridge College of Art
1988	Gastdozentin am Maidstone College und der Byam Shaw School of Art, London

EINZELAUSSTELLUNGEN

1983	LYC Museum & Art Gallery, Cumbria
1984	Minories Gallery, Colchester; Brewhouse Art Centre, Taunton; Festival Gallery, Bath; Blackfriars Art Centre, Lincs.
1985	Lady Lodge Art Centre, Peterborough
1986	Collective Gallery, Edinburgh
	Battersea Arts Centre, London
	Camden Arts Centre, London
1987	Serpentine Gallery, London
1988	Chisenhale Gallery, London
	Mappin Gallery, Sheffield
	Wolverhampton Art Gallery
1989	Woodlands Gallery, Greenwich
	Elephant Trust and Greenwich Arts Council Awards
	1. Preis der "The Great Hurricane Sculpture Competition", Brighton

GRUPPENAUSSTELLUNGEN (Auswahl)

1981	"The London Group", South London Gallery; Royal Academy
1982	"The London Group", Camden Arts Centre
1983	"On Site", International Sculpture Symposium, Yorkshire Sculpture Park
1984	"Eaumages" Festival of Installations, Villedieu Cultural Centre, Paris
1985	Major Award, Portland Clifftop Sculpture Park, Dorset "Portland Documentation Exhibition", Southampton City Art Gallery; "Riverside Open", Riverside Studios, London
1986	Brixton Art Gallery, London; Artspace, Aberdeen; Hire Scheme, City Museum & Art Gallery, Peterborough; Museum in Lodz Polen
1987	"Springing Alive", Manchester City Art Galleries; "Sculpture in Scarborough", Scarborough Art Gallery; Unit Seven Gallery, London; Greater London Arts Award
1988	Sculpture Residency, Glasgow Garden Festival
1989	Royal National Rose Society Sculpture Exhibition, St. Albans; "3 D 89", zwei große Arbeiten für den Gunnersbury Park und die Watermans Gallery, London
1990	"Passages – Übergänge" Installationen und Skulpturen (mit Christine Merton, Elena Gaputyte und Diane Maclean), Pfalzgalerie Kaiserslautern

PUBLIKATIONEN

1982	Artists Newsletter, Arts Review;
1985	Artists Newsletter, Arts Review;
1986	Mel Gooding. Edward Gage. The Scotsmann; Margaret Garlake, Art Monthly;
1988	Artists Newsletter, Emme Dexter, Artswork; Art Monthly; File Magazine; WASL Journal; Arts Review; Robert Clarke, The Guardian;
1989	Arts Review (March & July).

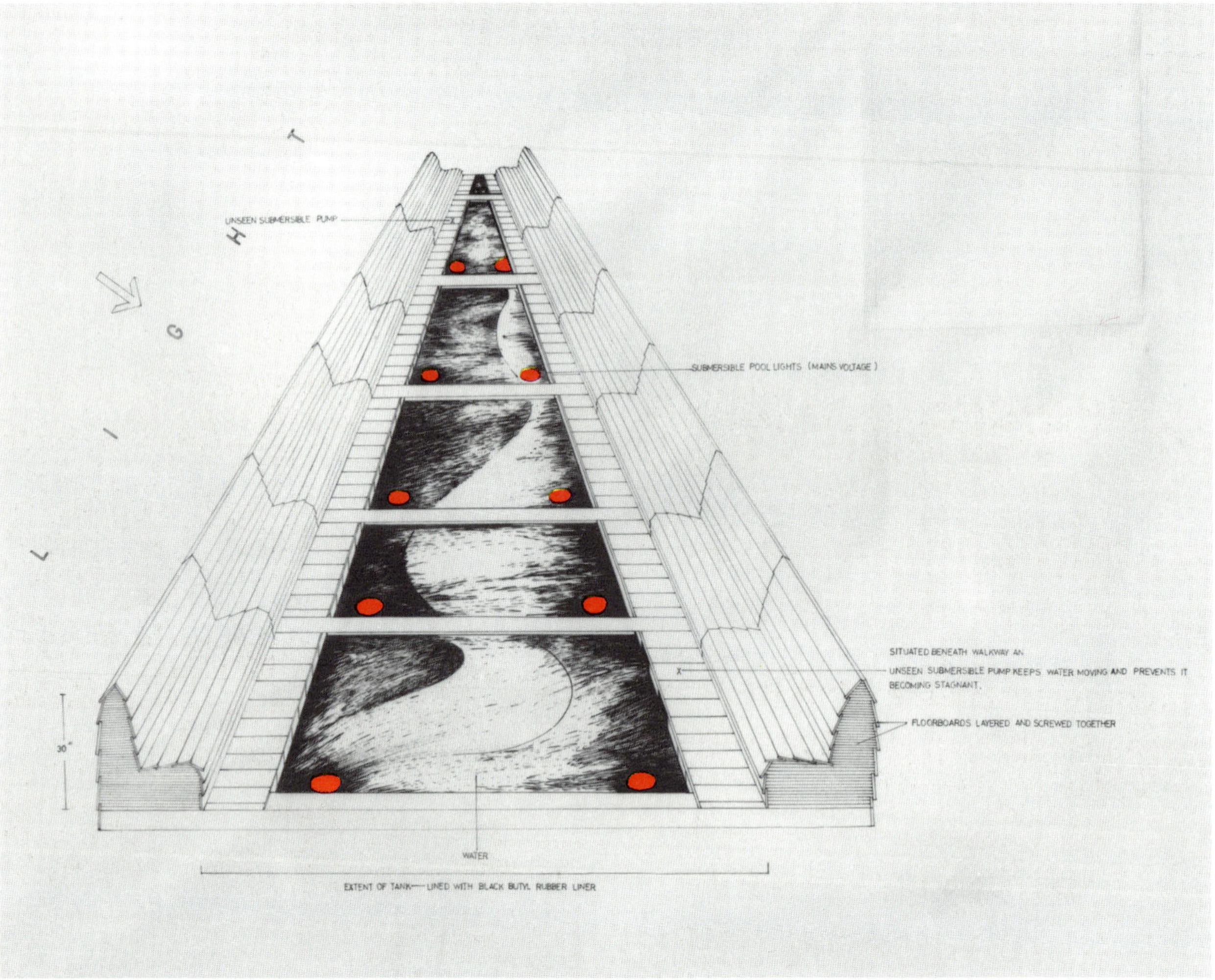

☐ XO, 1791, 1990
Holz, Gummiplane, Lampen, Elektromotoren
76 x 1220 x 616 cm

Wreck, 1984/85
Röntgenaufnahmen, Äste, Seile
211 x 216 x 640 cm

Portland Wreck, 1985
Steine, Wasser, Erde, Eisenbahnschwellen
200 x 625 x 19 cm

Forensic Evidence, 1987
Gerüstbretter
75 x 240 x 980 cm

Wake (Detail), 1987/88
Asche, Blei
1980 x 1150 cm

Wake, 1987/88

Wake, 1987/88

False Floor (3), 1988
Gerüst-Bretter und Wannen
77 x 390 x 390 cm

Floating Floor, 1989
Holz, Wasser
460 x 460 x 60 cm

Doorway, 1989
Holz, Wasser
35 x 195 x 174 cm

Bowl, 1989, Gunnersbury Park, London
Erde, Rasen, Holz, Eisen
800 x 800 x 100 cm

Diane Maclean

"And what we think, a breathing like the wind,
A moving part of a motion, a discovery
Part of a discovery, a change part of a change,
A sharing of colour and being part of it."

Wallace Stevens

DIANE MACLEAN

1939	geboren in London
	lebt in London
1956 - 58	Sprachstudium am University College, London. Abschluß als Bachelor of Arts
1960 - 76	Lebt in Belgien und Afrika. Verschiedene Ausstellungen, Porträtaufträge
1980 - 85	Studium am Hertfordshire College of Art & Design. Bachelor of Arts
1986	Zeichnungsprojekt für Silsden, West Yorkshire
1988	Lehrauftrag am Hertfordshire College of Art & Design
1990	Mitglied des Ausschusses für bildende Künste, Eastern Arts Association

AUSSTELLUNGEN (Auswahl)

1983	Six Sculptors, The Sculpture Walk, Great Linford, Milton Keynes
1984	Drawing for All, Gainsborough's House, Sudbury
	Moving On, Hertfordshire College of Art & Design
	100 Artists Show, The Showroom, Bonner Road, E 1
1985	Sculpture in the Garden Landscape, Probus, Cornwall
1986	New Contemporaries, ICA, London; Hatton Gallery, Newcastle; Bluecoat & Hanover Galleries, Liverpool
	Drawing for All, Gainsborough's House, Sudbury
1987	The Civic Centre, St. Albans
	The Crypt, St. George's, Bloomsbury, WC 1
	Women & Humour, Hammersmith Town Hall, London
	Coastlines, Towner Art Gallery & Museum, Eastbourne; The Pavilion, Leeds
	Ravenscourt Park. Wood sculpture project
	The Civic Trust Exhibition, Business Design Centre, Islington
1988	Festival '88, St. Albans City Centre, April ist the Cruellest Month
	Eliot College, University of Kent at Canterbury
	Dixon Gallery, Institute of Education, London University
	The Library, Exeter University
	The King's Manor, York University
1989	The King's Manor, York University
	Hertfordshire Ausstellung
	Sculpture in a Rose Garden: Royal National Rose Society
1990	"Passages – Übergänge" Installationen und Skulpturen (mit Christine Merton, Rosie Leventon und Elena Gaputyte), Pfalzgalerie Kaiserslautern

PUBLIKATIONEN

Women Artists Slide Library Journal, April/May 1987, August/Sept. 1987, April/May 1988; Options Magazine, July 1987; The Third Degree, Exeter University Magazine, Oct 1988; Western Morning News, John Onsley, Nov. 1988; Yorkshire Art Scene, Feb. 1989; April is the Cruellest Month, Ausstellungskatalog A. D. Moody 1988; Arts Review, July 1989, 'Sculpture in a Rose Garden', Mary Rose Beaumont; Vasari, Autumn 1989

☐ Three Sea Pieces, 1989
Muslin, Holz, Aluminium
660 x 100 cm

Fall, 1989
Holz, Stahl, Draht
340 x 900 cm

☐ Fall, 1989

☐ Wave, 1989
Japanpapier, blaues Holz, Wind
285 x 650 cm

☐ Wave, 1989

In Exile, 1985
Holz
120 x 122 x 70 cm

Littoral (S'ode ancora il mare), 1985
215 x 360 cm
Japanpapier, Sand, Holz, Wind

Tress, 1989
Aluminium
Höhe: 400 cm

Slate Sculpture II, 1985
Steinplatten
Länge: 392 cm

Shoal, 1985
Aluminium, Holz
183 x 213 x 153 cm

Stranded Head, 1986
Stahl
137 x 215 x 132 cm

Christine Merton

„. . . . . Und wenn du eintrittst, bist du Gast. – Bei wem?”

„. . . . . And when you enter, you are guest. – Of whom?” – Rainer Maria Rilke

Drei Zelte: Die Wand
Das Wort
Das Gewand

Es gibt eine ägyptische Hieroglyphe, die ein Zelt darstellt. Es bezieht sich auf die Seele als „Körper der Seligkeit”, welche den Geist wie ein Zelt umhüllt.

Three tents: The Wall
The Word
The Robe

There is an Egyptian hieroglyphic sign depicting the tent. This refers to the soul as a "body of glory" surrounding the spirit like a tent.

Die Wand · The Wall, 1989/90
Tuch, Farbe, Stahl, Backsteine
130 x 350 x 400 cm

□ Die Wand · The Wall, 1989/90

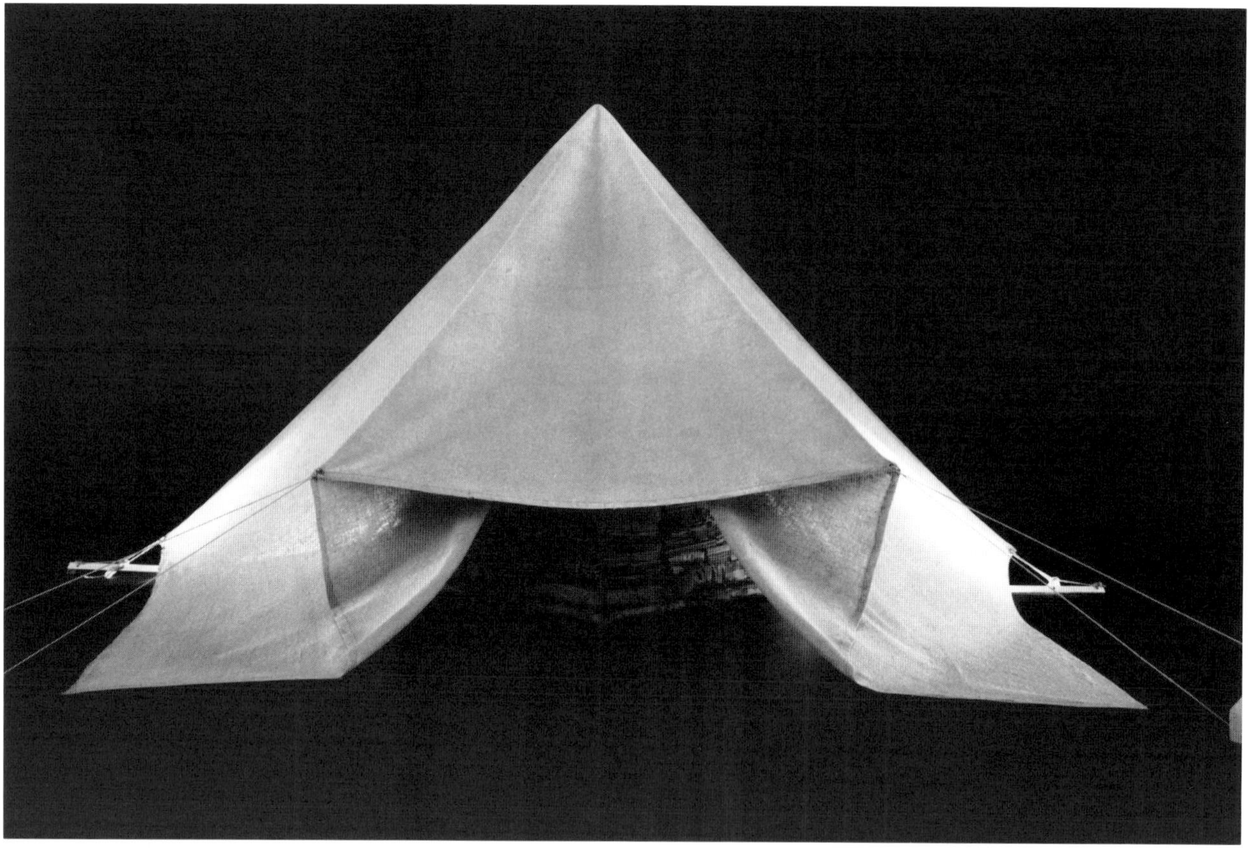

Das Wort · The Word, 1989/90
Tuch, Farbe, Stahl, Zeitungen
180 x 400 x 400 cm

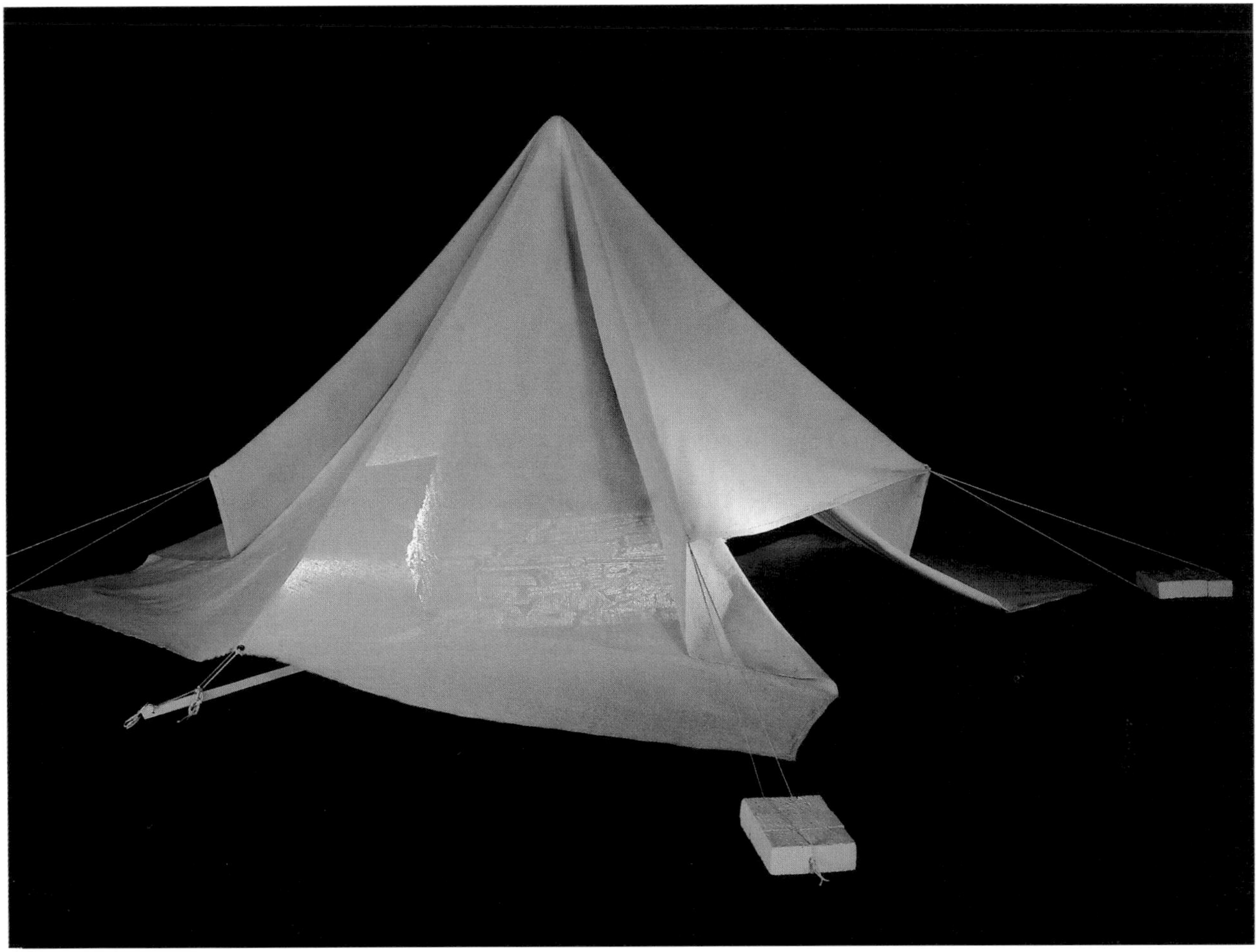

Das Wort · The Word, 1989/90

☐ Das Gewand · The Robe, 1989/90
Tuch, Farbe, Stahl, Plastik
250 x 300 x 300 cm

Das Gewand · The Robe, 1989/90

Vessel, 1988 (für das Manchester Museum)
Zweige, Sackleinen, Terracotta, Kiesel
ø 600 cm

Tree Tomb, 1988
Dachbalken, Reisig, Blätter
230 x 305 x 170 cm

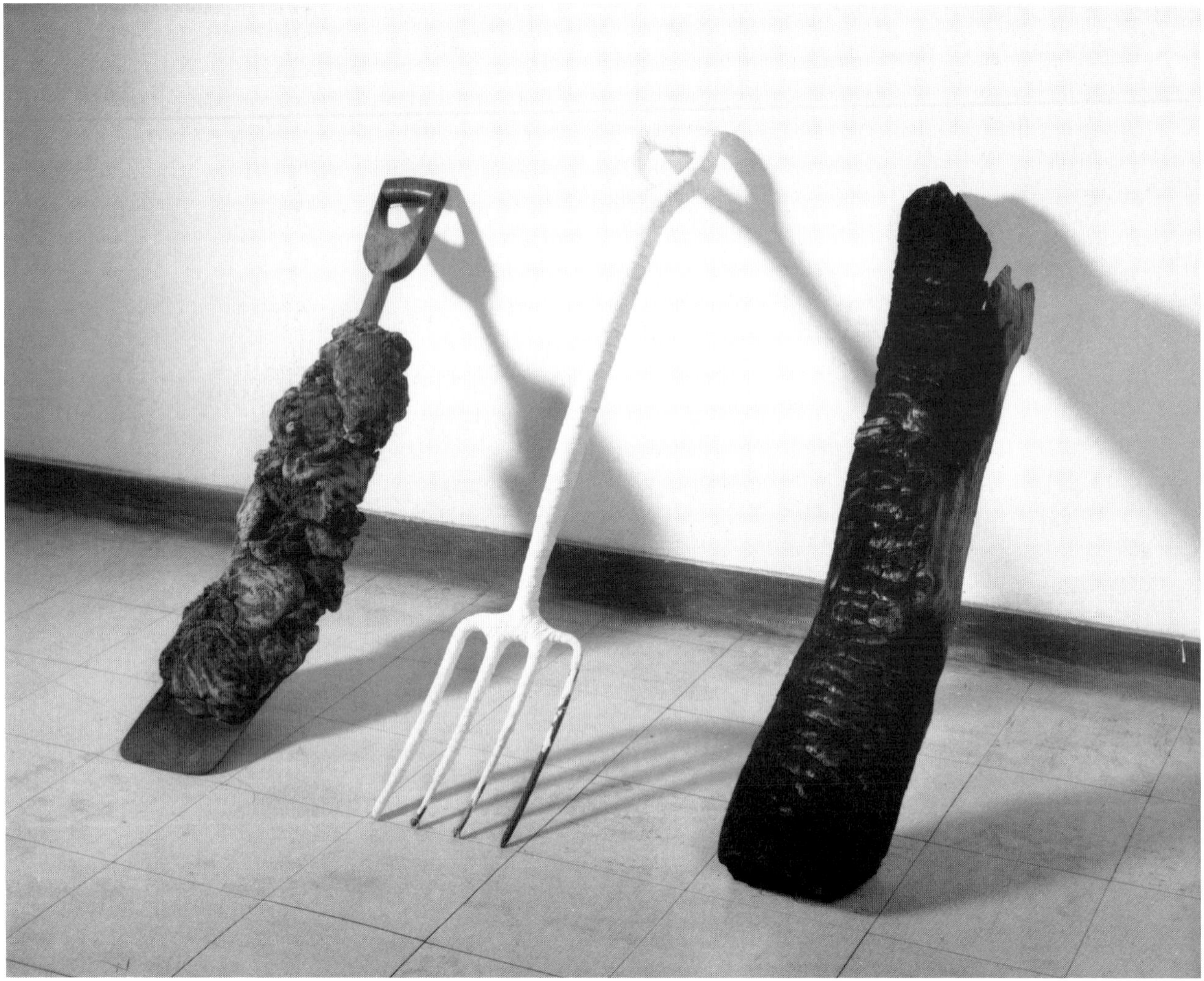

Three in One, 1989
Stahl, Holz, Ton, Gips
90 x 108 x 20 cm

Door between, 1989
Ton, Holz, Stahl
40 x 100 x 132 cm

CHRISTINE MERTON

1925	geboren in Plön/Holstein
	lebt in London
1959 - 62	Studium der Malerei an der Chelsea School of Art, London
1964	Weiterbildung bei Karl-Friedrich Gotsch in Deutschland
1972 - 75	Keramikkurs an der Sir John Cass School of Art, London
1975 - 80	Lehrauftrag am Camden Arts Centre, London
1976 - 88	Gastdozentin an der Sir John Cass School of Art; Artist in Residence and Commission an der Tolworth School for Girls; Mitglied des British Craft Index; Artist in Residence am Manchester Museum; Artist in Residence am Wigan Education Art Center in Drumcroon.

EINZELAUSSTELLUNGEN

1976	Sloane Street Gallery, London
1978	Galerie am Palmengarten, Frankfurt
1980	Oxford Gallery, Oxford (mit Merlyn Evans)
1981	Camden Art Centre, London
1983	Pfalzgalerie Kaiserslautern
1985	University of Kent, Canterbury
1986	South Hill Park Arts Centre, Bracknell (mit Roger Perkins)
	Axiom Centre for the Arts, Cheltenham
1988	Castlefield Gallery, Manchester, Manchester Museum; Royal Institute of British Architects; Drumcroon, Wigan Education Art Centre
1989	The London College of Furniture; Crescent Arts Workshop, Scarborough; Morley Gallery, London; Turnpike Gallery, Leigh, Gt. Manchester (mit Elizabeth Stuart-Smith); Gainsborough's House, Sudbury Exhibition & Residence.

GRUPPENAUSSTELLUNGEN

1980	"Clay Sculpture", Yorkshire Sculpture Park
1984	"A New View in the Garden", Oxford Gallery; Camden Annual, Camden Arts Centre; "London Group", Royal College of Art, London
1985	European Ceramics and Wall Textures, Fitzwilliam Museum, Cambridge
1987	"London Group", Royal College of Art, London; Sculpture in Scarborough
1989	Sculpture in a Rose Garden, Royal National Rose Society; Riverside Artists Group, Riverside Studios, London
1990	„Passages – Übergänge" Installationen und Skulpturen (mit Rosie Leventon, Diane Maclean und Elena Gaputyte), Pfalzgalerie Kaiserslautern

KUNST AM BAU

Tolworth School for Girls, London
Bad Homburg
Aachen

PUBLIKATIONEN

Arts Review, 1978, Jan/Febr, Oct 1981, 1984, 1986; Craft 1978, 1980; Kunst und Handwerk 1983; Art Line 1986; Women Artists Slide Library Journal, 1988; "Art for Nature" World Wildlife Trust; Ceramics Monthly, 1989; "Approaching Art & Design in Education", Rod Taylor Longman.

BEZIRKS
VERBAND
PFALZ

Impressum:
Ausstellung und Katalog:
Pfalzgalerie Kaiserslautern
Ausstellungstechnik:
Karl Anstäth, Wolfgang Kurrasch, Alois Schneider
Fotos: Künstlerinnen
Lithos: Repro 55, Trier – Druckhaus Roch KG, Kaiserslautern
Druck: Druckhaus Roch KG Kaiserslautern

ISBN 3-89422-030-9